For Chloe Montgomery • Stephanie Jeffs

For my Mum and Dad • Susan Wintringham

IN THE BEGINNING

By Stephanie Jeffs

Illustrated by
Susan Wintringham

Abingdon Press

I N THE BEGINNING THERE WAS NOTHING.

So God made the universe. It was empty, dark and lifeless. God said, "Let there be light!" And light appeared, so that there was light and there was darkness.

God made light travel faster than anything else in the universe. He made the dazzling white light run powerfully in a straight line. When it struck the earth it scattered in all directions. God split the light and it fragmented into colors: red, orange, yellow, green, blue, indigo and violet.

God made the light into day and the darkness into night. God made morning and he made evening. God made the first day.

God looked at all that he had made, and saw that it was good.

G OD GAVE THE EARTH SHAPE AND FORM.

God took the waters and divided and separated them until he had made the sky.

God wrapped the sky like a blanket around the earth, surrounding it with air. God made the air of gases: oxygen, carbon dioxide and nitrogen, and he made some of the water into clouds. God made a space ready to contain life.

God looked at all that he had made out of nothing, and saw that it was good.

GOD TOOK THE WATERS AND MOVED THEM.

God set the waters in their places, and made the seas cover two thirds of the earth with dry land in between.

God made the seas move. God made the waters flow in broad ocean currents and tiny ripples. He made them salty and full of minerals. God made it possible for the seas to influence the earth's climate and formed them to sustain life.

God made an undersea landscape with mountains and valleys, and he formed the dry land in the same way. God made the earth out of different kinds of rock, some hard like granite and basalt, and some soft like limestone and clay. God made sandstone crumbly and put holes in pumice.

Deep in the earth, God made it very hot. He made the rocks melt, alter their shape and change under pressure. He made them crystallize and form beautiful minerals, such as sapphires and diamonds. God made the surface of the earth move making volcanoes burst through.

God made all the trees and plants.

God made the plants and trees able to soak up the light he had made, taking in carbon dioxide from the air to make food and grow, and giving out oxygen. God made the trees dig their roots deep into the soil to drink in the water which had fallen as rain from the clouds.

God gave the trees different shapes. God made each leaf with a particular pattern and bark with a unique design.

God made each tree able to reproduce itself by bearing fruit with seeds inside. God made the fruit of the sycamore winged and spinning, and gave the orange tree sweet and juicy fruit inside a bitter skin.

God made mangrove trees grow on stilt-like roots on the edge of swamps. God made the trunk of the baobab tree which shrinks in the heat of the sun and swells with the rain. God made the conifers that survive the icy winds and snow, and the broad-leaved oak and elm that flourish in mild summers and cool winters. God made the redwood trees tower over all the trees around them. And on each redwood God placed cones and in the cones he put seeds. Each small seed could start a new tall tree.

G OD MADE PLANTS WITH FLOWERS.

God made some plants produce seeds and others produce spores. God gave the dandelion feathery parachute seeds, and made edible seeds such as peas and mustard. God gave spores to the unfurling ferns and the sprouting mushrooms.

God made all plants able to make their own food from the energy produced by the light he had made.

God made seaweed, red, brown and green, to float and grow in the seas. God gave them pockets of air to keep afloat and an anchor to help secure them to the rocks.

God made the cactus store water in its stem to grow in the heat of the desert. God made the leaves of the edelweiss thick and hairy to trap in warmth and grow on snowy mountain slopes.

God made wheat and barley and rice. He made cola nuts and cocoa beans, sweetcorn and sweet potatoes, apples and pineapples, strawberries, blueberries and blackberries.

God made cotton plants with fluffy seedheads, and aloe vera plants which produce soothing oil. God made the bark of the cinchona tree which produces bitter-tasting quinine.

God saw that all he had made was good.

GOD MADE ORDER IN THE UNIVERSE.

God placed the earth close to the sun. He trapped it in orbit by the force of gravity.

God made the earth move around the sun giving the earth years and seasons, times of heat and times of cold. God made the earth rotate as it moved around the sun, giving days and nights. He made the sun give warmth and light to the earth by day, and put the moon close to the earth to reflect the sun's light at night.

God made other planets to go around the sun. He made two other rocky planets to go between the sun and the earth: Mercury with its many craters, and Venus, the hottest planet of all. God made Mars with its dust storms and cold temperatures, and giant Jupiter, with its center of melted rock and sixteen moons. God made the rings of ice that surround Saturn, and gave Uranus clouds of blue methane gas. God made stormy Neptune and, furthest from the sun, icy Pluto, the smallest planet in the solar system. God placed the sun and all its planets with millions more stars in the Milky Way. He placed the stars in constellations that decorated the vastness of the night sky.

God looked at all that he had made out of nothing, and saw that it was good.

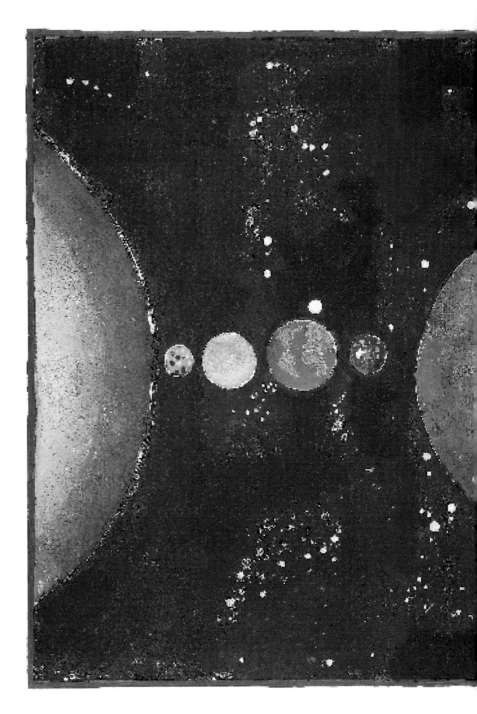

GOD FILLED THE OCEANS AND THE SKY WITH LIFE.

The air and the sea became alive with living creatures of every description. God made the sea bed home to sea anemones, brittlestars, prawns, crabs and sea horses. Nearer the surface of the water God made dolphins and whales rise and sink in the salty sea. He made the dolphins click and the whales sing.

God made freshwater eels and deep-sea slickheads. God made flying fish, the fast streamlined tuna, and the flat flounder which lies unnoticed on the muddy seabed. He made the huge blue whale the largest creature in the seas and the tiny sea anemone one of the slowest.

God made the stickleback which builds nests of twigs, and the bullhead which builds muddy burrows out of the soft ocean floor. God created the gourami which makes a floating raft of bubbles to nest in.

And God gave each sea creature a way of making more of its own kind so they would fill the seas. He made the sea gooseberry produce eggs and sperm to join in the water and grow into more sea gooseberries. He made male and female herrings work together to produce hundreds of tiny herring. He made the young blue shark grow inside its mother before being born into the sea.

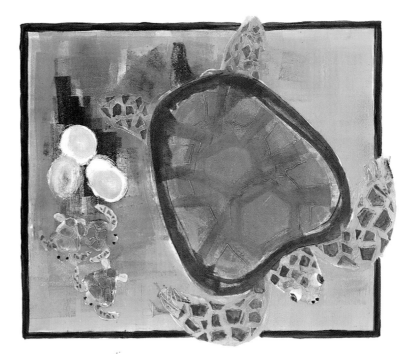

G OD CREATED BIRDS TO FILL THE SKY.

God covered their bodies with feathers, and gave them plumage of many different colors and patterns.

To some, like the eagle, God gave good eyesight and hearing; to others, like the hummingbird, God gave speed and color; and to yet more, like the albatross, God gave stamina and strength.

God made laughing kookaburras and whistling ducks, screech owls, song thrushes and snore rails. He filled the world with the sound of kittiwakes, curlews, babblers, warblers, chiff-chaffs, whippoorwills and cuckoos.

God made male and female birds. He made the head of the female goosander rusty red and the male goosander's head green. God gave the peacock a fan of bright tail feathers and the peahen brown feathers so she can hide easily. God made the female peregrine larger than the male. But he made the pairs of black and white oystercatchers look all alike.

God gave the great crested grebes a dance to help each one choose its mate.

GOD CREATED LAND BIRDS AND WATER BIRDS.

God made the pelican and the flamingo with sieve-like beaks, so that they could catch fish and strain off water, and the humming bird with a beak like a drinking straw. God gave the toucan and the puffin bold and brightly colored beaks.

God made the long-billed spider hunter which nests under a leaf to protect it from the sun. God made the common kingfisher which tunnels in the side of the river bank, and the male weaver bird which hangs its grassy nest from the branch of a tree.

God made the female birds able to produce eggs when they mate. He gave round eggs to the owls and long eggs to the swallows. God made the eggs blue, brown, speckled, each one colored and patterned so that it would lie unseen in its nest. Inside the eggs God made the chicks grow. He formed tiny legs and wings, beaks and toes, eyes and feathers. In the condor's egg he made a young condor, from the wren's egg he brought a new wren.

God knew all the creatures he had made, both in the sea and in the sky. As God looked at all that he had made out of nothing, he saw that it was good.

GOD CREATED CREATURES GREAT AND SMALL.

God covered the ground with creatures that crawl. He made every type of reptile, from the largest to the smallest. God designed the slender-necked diplodocus and the three-horned triceratops. He made tortoises, lizards, alligators and snakes. He made them scuttle, scramble and slither across the earth, swim in the cool waters of the sea, drink from the rivers and bask in the warmth of the sun.

God made sheep covered in warm wool and cows which produce plenty of milk. He made hungry goats and gobbling pigs. He made horses swift, donkeys strong and llamas safe and steady.

God made insects. He made more kinds of insects than of anything else. He made caterpillars that could grow into green mountain swallowtails and purple emperor butterflies. He made bumble bees by the nestful and tower-building termites.

God made the black widow spider and the scurrying scorpion.

GOD CREATED EVERY KIND OF ANIMAL.

God made animals of many kinds: rodents, apes, bears and antelopes. God made many kinds of antelope: the kudu and the impala, the eland, oryx and gazelle. God even made different kinds of gazelle: the jumping springbok and the long-necked dibatag.

He made the cheetah to be the fastest, the giraffe to be the tallest, and the elephant to be the largest mammal on the land.

God made the hyena grunt and whine and laugh and he gave the howler monkey the loudest sounds of all.

God made the otter with web-like flippers and gave the sloth strong arms to hang upside down. He made the flying gecko and flying dragon to glide from branch to branch, and he made the chameleon able to become lighter and darker to blend in with its surroundings.

God made the leafy forest home to the woodchuck and the roe deer, and the golden lion tamarin monkey to live in the rain forest.

God made every species of animal reproduce more of its own kind. He made rats produce tiny rats, blind and helpless. He made female koalas carry small koalas around in their pouches. He made polar bears slide down the ice playing with their cubs.

GOD CREATED MAN AND WOMAN.

God looked at all that he had made, and knew that he had yet to make a very special part of his creation. God said, "I will create people. They will be like me. They will be able to create new things with what I have made. They will have ideas and they will speak. I will place them in charge of the world. And just like me, they will be able to love and care for all that I have made."

So, just as God had created male and female of the fish and insects, birds and animals, he created man and woman. And he told them to have children so that there would be many people. He wanted them to live all over the world, on the mountains and in the valleys, in the hot deserts and jungles, and in the places where snow covered the earth. He wanted them to eat what the earth produced, to govern his world and to care for it.

God looked at all that he had made out of nothing, and saw that it was very good.

G OD RESTED WHEN HIS CREATION WAS FINISHED.

God had made the earth, and given it land and sea. God had filled the universe with solar systems, stars and galaxies. God had created time, with days, years and seasons. God had hidden rocks and minerals deep within the earth. God had created life, and filled the earth, sea and skies with living creatures of every kind.

God had made spiders, spider monkeys and spider crabs. He had made red, grey and flying squirrels, and blackbirds, black bears and black holes. God had made the blue-ringed octopus, the blue whale and the bluebottle fly as well as honey, honey badgers and honey creepers. He had made stars, starfish and starlings, as well as water boatmen, water lilies and waterfalls. God had made light and dark, sweet and sour, wet and dry, hot and cold, rough and smooth.

And God had created people, man and woman, to be a reflection of himself, able to love and to be loved.

God looked at all that he had made out of nothing, and saw that it was very good.

A Tamarind Book
Published in the United States of America by
Abingdon Press
P.O. Box 801
Nashville, TN 37202-0801
U.S.A
ISBN 0-687-08730-9

First edition 1997

Printed and bound in Singapore